Marvelous Morsels

Unique food gifts for year-round giving

Maggie Ruth Smith

Marvelous Morsels

Unique food gifts for year-round giving

This cookbook is a collection of favorite recipes,
which are not necessarily original recipes.

Published by McMichael-Kidd
Copyright © 2001 by
Maggie Ruth Smith
1553 Fountain Grove Road
Morrison, Tennessee 37357

ISBN: 0-9704331-0-7
LC Control Number: 00-092705

Cover Illustration: Mrs. Beulah Jean Hill Crownover

Edited, Designed, and Manufactured by
Favorite Recipes® Press

FRP

P.O. Box 305142
Nashville, Tennessee 37230
800-358-0560

Book Design: Jim Scott
Art Director: Steve Newman
Project Manager: Ginger Dawson

Manufactured in the United States of America

First Printing: 2001   6,000 copies

Dedication

To: Makinna Bronson Corbin

God danced the day you were born

(and so did I)

Acknowledgments

TO THOSE WHO HAVE GIVEN ME THE GIFT OF FOOD:
Tammy Algood, Mary Anne Best, Gail Bible, Sherry Dillard Bryant, Sherrie Smith Corbin, Louise Durman, Anita Barton Goodman, Addean Walker Fletcher, Doris Liles, Betty Harrell, Marilyn Henry, Brenda McPheeters, Edwina Pate, Duwana Powers, Mildred Powers, Janey Ruth Price, Judy Mitchell, Christine Freeze Smith, Maggie Sue McMichael Smith, Margaret Chappell Smolka, Maymie Kidd Spears, Arlene Voecks, and *Alesia Walden.* I thank you.

TO THE STAFF OF FRP: You have been most helpful and your encourage-ment never ceasing. You have truly bolstered my ego. To *Ginger Ryan Dawson,* my project leader, thank you for "championing the cause" to work with me. Your confidence in this project truly flattered me.

To *Ann Hazlewood,* whose gifts of food and friendship helped this book flow much easier. Thanks for being my sounding board. To *Bonnie McPheeters,* whose editing of ancillary text was most helpful. A special thank you to *Mrs. Beulah Jean Hill Crownover,* not only for her illustrations but, most importantly, for her prayers. To *Jannie:* thanks for putting the pen to the paper. To *Dad:* thanks for the encouragement every step of the way. To *Mom:* thanks for simply taking care of me. To *Bucket:* thanks for just being you. And to the *One* who always sustains me, I am truly humbled and nourished by You.

Table of Contents

About the Author

Marvelous Morsels is the author's first foray into publishing. A graduate of both Tennessee Technological University and the University of Tennessee at Knoxville, Ms. Smith holds three degrees in agriculture. She has conducted research on a variety of food products: eggs, meats, canned and frozen foods, confectioneries, and produce. Many of the products she has developed are available at the retail level. In addition to accomplishments in research and development and quality assurance, Ms. Smith has worked with the Tennessee Department of Agriculture "Pick Tennessee Products" campaign. She has written articles and developed radio and television segments featuring food product information. Her most illustrious accomplishment to date is that of cancer survivor.

Maggie Smith always wanted to write a cookbook, not for fame or glory, she says, but for mere self-gratification. In 1999, Ms. Smith was diagnosed with cancer, and three and a half months later she survived an automobile accident that could have been a fatality. Realizing life is indeed short and knowing she is still alive for a purpose, she says she decided to throw caution and skepticism to the wind and write a cookbook.

The concept for Marvelous Morsels was developed when Ms. Smith began having problems knowing what gifts to buy for family and friends. She wanted an alternative to the stress that often comes with shopping for gifts. Since everyone can use and enjoy food gifts, Ms. Smith compiled these recipes, complete with some unique packaging suggestions, that you can prepare for friends and loved ones—gifts the recipient will know came from the heart.

Introduction

When I think of food it brings to mind wonderful memories. I remember sitting on the front porch with a glass of ice tea talking with friends or sipping lemonade at twilight listening to the sounds of nature. Some of my fondest memories are of sitting around the kitchen table enjoying not only the food but the fellowship of friends and family. The kitchen table was always piled high with chicken, macaroni and cheese, mashed potatoes, green beans, and all those other "stick-to-your-ribs" dishes. In the summer, a plate of freshly sliced tomatoes took center stage, and no matter the time of year a variety of desserts was always available.

Food has always been an integral part of my life, and I think it is so with most southerners. We use food as the bond to bring people together. Whether in a time of grief, crisis, celebration, or fellowship, food is comfort and is nourishment, not only for the body, but for the soul as well.

Food gifts come from the heart. They evoke feelings of warmth and caring. They are the gift in which you give part of yourself. *Marvelous Morsels* is filled with recipes intended to soothe and nourish the mind, body, and soul. It is my hope you will use these recipes to be the ties that bind people together.

Maggie Ruth Smith

Spring is a time of revitalization and awakening. It is the time to renew friendships, to break out of the mold, and to find your hidden spirit. It is a season of showers, flowers, and energy. Spring is Easter, May Day, graduations, and honoring parents. It is fresh fruit with white chocolate sauce, snack mix for a hike, and balsamic vinaigrette for a citrus salad.

It is marinated mushrooms, spring vegetable spread, and spoon rolls for a busy friend. It is fresh salad dressings for the gardens' bounty. It is dipping sauces, mixes, and condiments. Spring is fresh, as fresh as the air after a rain.

Contents

Marinated mushrooms

PACKAGE THESE MUSHROOMS WITH COLORFUL WOODEN PICKS
FOR SERVING.

2/3 cup vegetable oil
1/3 cup wine vinegar
1 tablespoon chopped parsley
1 tablespoon lemon juice
1 garlic clove, chopped
1/4 to 1/2 teaspoon sugar
1/8 to 1/2 teaspoon pepper
Hot sauce to taste
2 pounds small fresh mushrooms

- Combine the oil, wine vinegar, parsley, lemon juice, garlic, sugar, pepper and hot sauce in a small bowl and mix well.
- Rinse the mushrooms and leave them whole; pat dry.
- Pour the oil mixture over the mushrooms in a serving dish, tossing to coat.
- Chill, covered, for 4 to 6 hours.

Yield: 10 servings

Mexicali cheese crackers

THE FLAVOR OF THESE CRACKERS IMPROVES WITH TIME. PREPARE THEM
1 TO 2 DAYS IN ADVANCE TO ALLOW THE FLAVORS TO BLEND.

1 (14-ounce) box cheese crackers
1/2 cup (1 stick) butter or margarine, melted
1 envelope taco seasoning mix
1 to 1 1/4 tablespoons Worcestershire sauce
1/8 to 1/2 teaspoon seasoned salt

- Pour the crackers into a gallon-size sealable plastic bag.
- Combine the melted butter, taco seasoning mix, Worcestershire sauce and seasoned salt in a small bowl and mix well.
- Pour over the crackers in the plastic bag. Shake to coat well.
- Spread the mixture on a baking sheet.
- Bake at 250 degrees for 1 hour, stirring every 15 minutes.
- Spread onto waxed paper to cool.
- Store in an airtight container.

Yield: 6 cups

spring

Tempting snack mix

4 cups mini shredded wheat cereal
1 (10-ounce) can sesame nut mix
2 cups pretzel sticks
½ cup (1 stick) margarine
2 tablespoons grated Parmesan cheese
1½ to 2 teaspoons oregano
1½ to 2 teaspoons basil
½ teaspoon garlic powder

- Combine the shredded wheat cereal, nut mix and pretzel sticks in a large bowl. Set aside.
- Combine the margarine, Parmesan cheese, oregano, basil and garlic powder in a saucepan.
- Cook over medium heat until the margarine is melted, stirring constantly.
- Pour the margarine mixture over the cereal mixture and mix to coat well.
- Spread the mixture on a baking sheet.
- Bake at 325 degrees for 20 minutes, stirring after 10 minutes.
- Let cool. Store in an airtight container.

Yield: 7 cups

Sweet mustard dip

THIS DIP IS GREAT WITH HAM AND TURKEY AS WELL AS WITH PRETZELS AND EGG ROLLS.

4 ounces sweetened condensed milk
1/4 cup prepared mustard
3 tablespoons prepared horseradish
1 tablespoon Worcestershire sauce
2 tablespoons sour cream (optional)

- Combine the sweetened condensed milk, mustard, horseradish, Worcestershire sauce and sour cream in bowl and mix until well blended.
- Store in an airtight container in the refrigerator.

The dip will thicken as it stands, so do not fret if it initially seems thin. Ground mustard may be used if a hotter dip is preferred.

Yield: 3/4 cup

spring

Italian spread

PACKAGE THIS SPREAD INTO A MOLD OR CROCK AND WRAP IN COLORED PLASTIC WRAP WITH A RIBBON. NOT ONLY ARE YOU GIVING A WONDERFUL SPREAD, BUT THE MOLD OR CROCK CAN BE REUSED. THIS IS ALSO A NICE SPREAD FOR BREAD.

8 ounces cream cheese, softened
1 envelope Italian salad dressing mix
⅔ cup mayonnaise

- Combine the cream cheese, dressing mix and mayonnaise in a small bowl.
- Mix until well blended.
- Chill, covered, until serving time.
- Serve with assorted crackers and fresh vegetables.

Yield: 1 cup

Spring vegetable spread

THIS SPREAD MAY BE PACKAGED IN A VARIETY OF WAYS. IT MAY BE PACKED INTO CROCKS OR SMALL GLASS FLOWERPOTS. YOU MAY ALSO SHAPE THE SPREAD INTO A LOG OR BALL AND ROLL IN PAPRIKA OR FINELY CHOPPED PECANS. BE CREATIVE AND ADD YOUR OWN COLORFUL, FESTIVE TOUCH.

1 package Knorr spring vegetable soup mix
24 ounces cream cheese, softened

- Combine the soup mix and cream cheese in a bowl.
- Mix until well blended.
- Chill, covered, for 24 hours to allow vegetable pieces to soften.
- Serve with assorted crackers or fresh vegetables.
- For smaller vegetable pieces, place the soup mix in a food processor container and pulse until desired consistency is reached.

For a variation, ¾ cup chopped nuts may be added to the spread.

Yield: 3 cups

Fruited cheese ball

8 ounces cream cheese, softened
2 ounces crumbled feta cheese
1/2 cup fruit preserves (any flavor)
1/4 cup chopped pecans

- Combine the cream cheese and feta cheese in a small bowl and mix until well blended.
- Stir in the fruit preserves and pecans.
- Shape into a ball and wrap in plastic wrap.
- Chill until serving time.

You may substitute walnuts for the pecans if desired.

For a variation, you may roll the cheese ball in the chopped nuts rather than mixing them into the cheese. The cheese ball may be prepared up to 5 days in advance. The flavor is best if it is prepared at least 3 days in advance.

Yield: 10 servings

Simple fruit salad

2 (15-ounce) cans pineapple chunks
1 (11-ounce) can mandarin oranges, drained
3 bananas, sliced
1 (3-ounce) package vanilla instant pudding mix
3 tablespoons orange breakfast drink mix
Chopped nuts to taste
Miniature marshmallows to taste

- Drain the pineapple and reserve the juice.
- Combine the pineapple, mandarin oranges and bananas in a bowl.
- Sprinkle the pudding mix over the fruit.
- Combine the reserved pineapple juice and orange breakfast drink mix in a small bowl and mix well.
- Pour the pineapple juice mixture over the fruit and mix well.
- Fold in chopped nuts and marshmallows.
- Chill, covered, until serving time.

Yield: 4 to 6 servings

spring

Balsamic vinaigrette

PACKAGE THIS DRESSING WITH A VARIETY OF SALAD GREENS,
ORANGES, AND GRAPEFRUIT TO MAKE A REFRESHING CITRUS SALAD.

1/3 cup honey
2 tablespoons balsamic vinegar
1/2 teaspoon salt
1/4 teaspoon pepper
1/4 cup olive oil

• Combine the honey, balsamic vinegar, salt and
  pepper in a small bowl and mix well.
• Add the olive oil gradually, whisking until
  well blended.
• Store in an airtight container in the refrigerator.
• Let stand at room temperature before serving.

Yield: 2/3 cup

spring

Bleu cheese dressing

THIS DRESSING IS BEST IF USED WITHIN 2 WEEKS.

1 cup mayonnaise
3/4 cup buttermilk
7 drops Tabasco sauce
1 teaspoon steak sauce
1 tablespoon Italian seasoning
1 tablespoon parsley flakes
1 garlic clove, minced
6 ounces bleu cheese, crumbled

- Combine the mayonnaise, buttermilk, Tabasco sauce and steak sauce in a bowl and whisk until well blended.
- Whisk in the Italian seasoning, parsley flakes and garlic.
- Fold in the bleu cheese. Store in an airtight container in the refrigerator.

Yield: 2 1/2 cups

Caesar dressing

THIS DRESSING IS BEST IF USED WITHIN 1 WEEK.

3/4 cup prepared Italian salad dressing
1/3 cup mayonnaise
1 to 2 tablespoons grated Parmesan cheese
1 tablespoon sugar
1 teaspoon soy sauce

- Combine the Italian dressing, mayonnaise, Parmesan cheese, sugar and soy sauce in a bowl and whisk until well blended.
- Store in an airtight container in the refrigerator.

Yield: 1 cup

spring

French dressing

1 medium onion, coarsely chopped
1 cup ketchup
3/4 cup vinegar
1 cup sugar
1 teaspoon salt
1 teaspoon paprika
1/4 teaspoon celery salt
1 garlic clove, chopped
1 1/2 cups peanut oil

- Place the onion in a blender container.
- Add the ketchup and vinegar and process until well blended.
- Add the sugar, salt, paprika, celery salt and garlic gradually, processing until well mixed.
- Add the peanut oil in a slow stream, processing until smooth.
- Store in an airtight container in the refrigerator.

Yield: 3 cups

Honey mustard dressing

PACKAGE THIS DRESSING IN A PRETTY BOTTLE WITH SEVERAL OTHER HOMEMADE DRESSINGS FOR A SPECIAL SPRINGTIME GIFT.

3/4 cup mayonnaise
3 tablespoons honey
3 tablespoons prepared yellow mustard
1 tablespoon lemon juice

- Combine the mayonnaise, honey, mustard and lemon juice in a bowl and mix until well blended.
- Chill, covered, for 4 hours before serving.

Yield: 1 cup

spring

Homemade mayonnaise

1 egg
1/2 cup vegetable oil
1 teaspoon prepared mustard
2 tablespoons lemon juice
1/2 teaspoon salt
1/4 teaspoon sugar
1 cup vegetable oil

- Combine the egg, 1/2 cup oil, mustard, lemon juice, salt and sugar in a blender container.
- Process until well blended. Add 1 cup oil in a slow stream, processing until smooth.
- Store in an airtight container in the refrigerator. This will keep for several weeks.

You may use egg substitute equivalent to 1 egg to avoid raw eggs that may carry salmonella.

Yield: 2 cups

Tangy onion dressing

THIS DRESSING IS BEST IF MADE AT LEAST 2 DAYS BEFORE SERVING. IT
WILL KEEP FOR SEVERAL WEEKS IN THE REFRIGERATOR.

1 to 2 Vidalia onions, chopped
2 teaspoons salt
2 teaspoons pepper
2 teaspoons dry mustard
2 teaspoons paprika
1/2 cup sugar
3/4 cup white vinegar
Vegetable oil

- Fill a quart jar half full of the chopped onions.
  Add the salt, pepper, dry mustard and paprika.
- Add the sugar and vinegar and mix well.
- Add enough oil to fill the jar and mix until
  well blended.
- Screw on a tight-fitting lid. Store in the
  refrigerator, shaking vigorously before serving.

Yield: 2 cups

Thousand island dressing

THIS DRESSING KEEPS WELL FOR A COUPLE OF WEEKS IN THE REFRIGERATOR.

1 cup mayonnaise
½ cup ketchup
1 tablespoon chopped pimento
2 to 3 tablespoons grated onion
½ green bell pepper, finely chopped

- Combine the mayonnaise, ketchup, pimento, onion and bell pepper in a small bowl and mix well.
- Chill, covered, for several hours before serving.

Yield: 1½ cups

spring

Honey mustard dipping sauce

This is a delicious dipping sauce for chicken, hot dogs, or any kind of appetizer.

Spicy brown mustard
Honey

- Combine equal amounts of mustard and honey in a bowl.
- Mix until well blended.
- Chill, covered, for at least 4 hours before serving.

Yield: variable

Horseradish sauce

This is the perfect gift for meat lovers. It is a great sauce for beef or chicken.

1 cup sour cream
2 tablespoons milk
1½ tablespoons prepared horseradish

- Combine the sour cream, milk and horseradish in a bowl and mix well.
- Chill, covered, until serving time.

Yield: 1 cup

Chicken tenders seasoning mix

⅔ cup flour
2 teaspoons paprika
1 to 1½ teaspoons basil
1 to 1½ teaspoons oregano
½ teaspoon garlic powder
½ teaspoon seasoning salt
¼ teaspoon freshly ground black pepper
⅛ teaspoon cayenne pepper

- Combine the flour, paprika, basil, oregano, garlic powder, seasoning salt, black pepper and cayenne pepper in a bowl and mix well.
- Store in an airtight container.

Yield: ⅔ cup seasoning mix
(enough for 8 to 12 chicken tender strips)

To prepare Chicken Tenders:
- Combine 8 to 12 chicken tender strips and enough buttermilk to cover in a glass dish.
- Marinate, covered, in the refrigerator for 15 minutes.
- Coat the chicken tenders with the seasoning mix.
- Deep-fry in hot oil until golden brown and chicken is cooked through.

spring

Hush puppy mix

3 cups self-rising cornmeal
3 cups self-rising flour
¼ cup sugar

- Combine the cornmeal, flour and sugar in a bowl and mix well.
- Store in an airtight container until ready to use.

To prepare Hush Puppies:
- Combine the mix, 3 beaten eggs and 1 to 2 chopped large onions in a bowl and mix well.
- Add enough milk to make a sticky batter.
- Drop by spoonfuls into hot oil in a deep fryer.
- Deep-fry until golden brown.
- Remove with a slotted spoon to paper towels to drain.

Yield: 12 to 15 servings

spring

Spoon rolls

THESE ROLLS ARE GREAT SERVED WITH ANY MEAL. PACKAGE THE
BATTER IN REASEALABLE CONTAINERS AND GIVE AS A GIFT TO ALL THE
BUSY PEOPLE YOU KNOW.

2 cups lukewarm water
1 envelope dry yeast
3/4 cup (1 1/2 sticks) margarine, melted and cooled
2 small eggs, beaten
1/4 cup sugar
4 cups self-rising flour

- Pour the water into a large mixing bowl.
- Sprinkle the yeast over the water and stir until the yeast is dissolved.
- Add the margarine, eggs and sugar and mix well.
- Add the flour and beat well until smooth. The batter will be fairly thick.
- Chill, covered, until ready to use. The batter will keep for 1 week in the refrigerator. Before preparing, stir the batter well. This batter improves after 1 or 2 days.

To prepare Spoon Rolls:
- Spoon the batter into greased muffin tins.
- Bake at 375 degrees for 10 minutes.

Yield: 3 dozen

Cream cheese bars

THIS IS A SCRUMPTIOUS GIFT FOR ANY TIME OF THE YEAR. YOU MAY CUT IT INTO LARGER PIECES TO SERVE AS A CAKE OR SMALLER SQUARES FOR BARS.

1 (2-layer) package yellow cake mix
1/2 cup chopped pecans
1/2 cup (1 stick) butter, softened
1 egg, beaten
1 (1-pound) package confectioners' sugar
8 ounces cream cheese, softened
2 eggs, beaten

- Combine the cake mix, pecans, butter and 1 egg in a mixing bowl and beat until well mixed.
- Press the mixture into the bottom of a 9×13-inch baking pan for the crust layer.
- Combine the confectioners' sugar, cream cheese and 2 eggs in a mixing bowl and beat until well blended.
- Pour over the top of the crust layer and smooth out evenly.
- Bake at 350 degrees for 35 to 40 minutes.
- Remove to a wire rack to cool. Let cool before cutting.

Yield: 15 to 20 servings

Jack Daniel's cake

2 cups flour
4 teaspoons baking powder
1/2 teaspoon salt
1 cup (2 sticks) butter
2 cups packed brown sugar
4 eggs, beaten
1/2 cup Jack Daniel's Tennessee Whiskey
1/4 cup water
6 ounces (1 cup) chocolate chips
1 cup chopped pecans
Butter Whiskey Glaze

- Combine the flour, baking powder and salt in a medium bowl; set aside.
- Melt the butter in a large saucepan over low heat.
- Remove from the heat and add the brown sugar, eggs, flour mixture, whiskey and water gradually, mixing well after each addition.
- Pour into a greased 9×13-inch cake pan.
- Sprinkle the chocolate chips and pecans evenly over the top.
- Bake at 325 degrees for 50 to 55 minutes or until a wooden pick inserted in the center of the cake comes out clean and the edges begin to pull away from the pan.
- Cool on a wire rack for 10 to 15 minutes. Drizzle with the Butter Whiskey Glaze.

Yield: 15 servings

Butter whiskey glaze

1/4 cup (1/2 stick) butter, melted
2 cups confectioners' sugar
1/3 cup Jack Daniel's Tennessee Whiskey
1 teaspoon vanilla extract

- Combine the melted butter, confectioners' sugar, whiskey and vanilla in a bowl and mix until well blended.

Blackberry cake

1 (2-layer) package white cake mix (with pudding in the mix)
1 (3-ounce) package blackberry gelatin
1 cup mashed blackberries
Cream Cheese Frosting

- Prepare the batter according to the package directions.
- Add the gelatin mix and mashed blackberries and mix well.
- Pour into a greased 9×13-inch cake pan.
- Bake according to the package directions.
- Remove to a wire rack to cool.
- Spread the Cream Cheese Frosting over the cooled cake.

You may substitute any flavor gelatin and fruit for the blackberry. Strawberry, peach and banana are especially good. Be sure and match the flavor of the gelatin with the fruit for optimum flavor.

Yield: 15 servings

Cream cheese frosting

8 ounces cream cheese, softened
½ cup (1 stick) margarine, softened
2 cups confectioners' sugar

- Combine the cream cheese and margarine in a mixing bowl. Beat until light and well blended.
- Add the confectioners' sugar and beat until of spreading consistency.

Easy fruit cobbler

ANY VARIETY OF FRUIT IS DELICIOUS IN THIS COBBLER.

1 cup sugar
1 cup self-rising flour
1 cup milk
½ cup (1 stick) butter or margarine, melted
1 (16-ounce) can fruit or pie filling

- Combine the sugar and flour in a large bowl. Add the milk and mix well. Add this mixture to the melted butter in a separate bowl and mix well.
- Spoon the fruit into an 8-inch square baking dish.
- Pour the batter over the fruit; do not mix.
- Bake at 350 degrees for 45 minutes or until bubbly and golden brown.

For a variation, add another can of fruit or pie filling and use a 9×13-inch baking dish. You will have a cobbler with more fruit than dough.

Yield: 6 servings

spring

Drunken cherries

THIS IS A COLORFUL GIFT WHEN PACKAGED IN A CLEAR JAR. THESE CHERRIES MAKE A DELICIOUS UNEXPECTED TREAT WHEN ADDED TO HOT OR COLD DRINKS SUCH AS A SINGAPORE SLING. GIVE A PLAIN FRUIT TRAY PANACHE BY ADDING THESE SPECIAL CHERRIES.

2 cups tart cherries, stems removed
1/2 cup sugar
1/2 cup water
1/4 to 1/2 cup brandy

- Place unpitted cherries in a heat-resistent 1-pint jar with a tight-fitting lid.
- Combine the sugar and water in a medium saucepan.
- Bring to a boil over high heat.
- Cook until the sugar is dissolved, stirring constantly.
- Cover and let boil for 2 minutes. Remove from the heat and stir in the brandy.
- Pour the hot syrup over the cherries in the jar. Seal the jar with the tight-fitting lid and refrigerate for at least 1 week and up to 3 months.
- Serve over cheesecake, ice cream or pound cake.

Yield: 2 cups

White chocolate sauce

PACKAGE THIS SAUCE WITH FRESH FRUIT AND HOMEMADE POUND CAKE FOR A DELICIOUS GIFT ANY TIME OF THE YEAR.

6 ounces (1 cup) white chocolate chips
1 cup sweetened condensed milk
1¼ cups heavy cream

- Combine the white chocolate chips and condensed milk in a saucepan over low heat.
- Cook until the chocolate chips are melted, stirring constantly.
- Remove from the heat and mix until well blended.
- Stir in the heavy cream.
- Chill, covered, until serving time.
- Serve with pound cake and your favorite fruit.

Try dipping pretzel sticks into the sauce while warm. Let cool and store in an airtight container or wrap in clear cellophane, tie with a ribbon, and give as a gift.

Yield: 3 cups

summer

Summer bursts onto the scene like a baseball player slides into base—full of fervor and gusto. The season is the elixir of life. Summer is Independence Day, Bastille Day, Labor Day, cookouts, and vacations compressed into three short months.

It is the season for giving gifts that cool the summertime stick. It is copper pennies for family gatherings, steak rub for cookouts, Sicilian olives for days at the lake, and sangria for evenings on the patio. It is fruit tea on the front porch, cream cheese spread with vine-ripened tomatoes, and peanut butter pie with homemade ice cream.

Summer is preparation. Preparation for less bountiful seasons. Preparation for year-round gift giving. It is canning salsa, making dill pickles, freezing orange blossoms, and creating rock candy. Summer is all about ease, simplicity and, most of all, enjoyment.

Contents

# Fruit tea

PACKAGE THE SUGAR AND DRINK MIXES ALREADY COMBINED IN A PINT JAR. PLACE THE JAR IN A BASKET WITH TEA BAGS AND MUGS. THIS TEA IS DELICIOUS SERVED HOT OR COLD.

> 5 cups water
> 4 family-size tea bags
> ¾ cup sugar
> ½ cup orange breakfast drink mix
> ½ cup lemonade drink mix
> Water

- Bring 5 cups of water to a boil in a saucepan. Add the tea bags and let boil for 15 seconds.
- Remove the pan from the heat and let the tea bags steep for 15 minutes.
- Combine the sugar and drink mixes in a 1-gallon container.
- Pour the tea into the container and mix well until the sugar and drink mixes are dissolved.
- Add enough water to fill the 1-gallon container.

Yield: 1 gallon (16 servings)

summer

Red sangria

PACKAGE ALL THE INGREDIENTS ALONG WITH THE RECIPE IN A NICE
BASKET. ADD WINE GLASSES AND YOU HAVE THE PERFECT GIFT.

2 oranges, sliced
2 lemons or limes (or 1 of each), sliced
2 apples, chopped
4 cups red wine
½ cup lemon juice
½ cup orange juice
1 (12-ounce) can lemon-lime soda

- Combine the oranges, lemons, apples and red wine in a large pitcher.
- Stir in the lemon juice and orange juice.
- Add the soda immediately before serving and mix well.
- This beverage is best if served within 2 to 3 days or the fruit will become too soggy.

Yield: 7 cups (6 to 8 servings)

summer

Feta spread

PACKAGE THIS SPREAD IN A PRETTY CROCK WITH FRESH LETTUCE, TOMATOES AND A LOAF OF FRESH WHITE BREAD. YOUR RECIPIENT WILL ONLY NEED TO SUPPLY THE BACON!

8 ounces cream cheese, softened
4 ounces feta cheese, softened
2 tablespoons each olive oil and balsamic vinegar
2 tablespoons basil
1 tablespoon chives

- Combine the cream cheese, feta cheese, olive oil, vinegar, basil and chives in a bowl and mix well.
- Chill, covered, for 4 hours or longer before serving.
- This spread will keep well for 7 days in the refrigerator.
- Serve on hot grilled vegetables or as a substitute for mayonnaise on BLTs.

Yield: 2½ cups

Compound butter

WRAP THE BUTTER IN WAXED PAPER AND TIE THE ENDS WITH COLORFUL RIBBON FOR A FESTIVE LOOK. PACKAGE WITH FRESH VEGETABLES OF THE SEASON OR HOMEMADE BREAD.

½ cup (1 stick) unsalted butter, softened
2¾ tablespoons assorted herbs

- Combine the butter and herbs in a small bowl and mix well.
- Shape into a log. Wrap the butter in plastic wrap and then wrap in waxed paper.
- Chill for 4 to 8 hours before serving.
- Serve on top of hot vegetables or grilled meats.

For a quicker method, roll the stick of butter in the herb mixture, wrap in plastic wrap and chill for at least 1 hour before serving.

Yield: 8 tablespoons

Cream cheese spread

PACKAGE THIS SPREAD IN A CROCK AND GIVE WITH A LOAF OF FRESH SOURDOUGH BREAD.

> 6 ounces cream cheese, softened
> 1/2 cup mayonnaise
> 3/4 teaspoon basil
> 1/8 teaspoon salt
> 1/8 teaspoon pepper

- Combine the cream cheese, mayonnaise, basil, salt and pepper in a bowl and mix well.
- Chill, covered, for at least 4 hours before serving.
- Spread on mini bread slices and top with a tomato slice for an easy appetizer.

This spread is also a great substitute for mayonnaise on a BLT.

Yield: 1 cup

summer

Pineapple fruit dip

SERVE THIS DIP IN A HOLLOWED-OUT PINEAPPLE FOR A BEAUTIFUL PRESENTATION. PACKAGE WITH FRUITS OF THE SEASON FOR A COOL AND REFRESHING GIFT.

1/2 cup sugar
2 tablespoons flour
1 egg, beaten
1 cup pineapple juice
8 ounces cream cheese, softened

- Combine the sugar, flour, egg and pineapple juice in a saucepan.
- Cook over low heat until thickened, stirring constantly.
- Remove from the heat.
- Beat in the cream cheese until well blended.
- Chill, covered, until serving time.
- Serve with a variety of fresh fruit.

Yield: 2 cups

Guacamole

PACKAGE THIS DIP WITH TORTILLA CHIPS AND VARIOUS SALSAS.

1 medium avocado, mashed
2 tablespoons minced onion (optional)
1 garlic clove, minced
2 tablespoons chopped fresh cilantro
1½ tablespoons salsa
1 tablespoon lemon or lime juice

- Combine the mashed avocado, onion, garlic, cilantro, salsa and lemon juice in a bowl and mix well.
- Chill, covered, until serving time.

This dip is best served within 2 days.

Yield: 1 cup

summer

Fresh salsa

PACKAGE THIS SALSA WITH TORTILLA CHIPS OR WITH THE INGREDIENTS
FOR TOPPING TACOS.

6 small ripe tomatoes, chopped
1 to 2 jalapeño chiles, seeded and minced
2 tablespoons minced onion
2 tablespoons chopped fresh cilantro or parsley
$1/4$ cup lemon or lime juice
1 teaspoon red wine vinegar
$1/8$ to $1/4$ teaspoon salt
$1/8$ to $1/4$ teaspoon pepper

- Combine the chopped tomatoes, chiles, onion,
  cilantro, lemon juice, vinegar, salt and pepper in
  a bowl and mix well.
- Chill, covered, until serving time.

*You may peel the tomatoes if desired. This salsa is
best if served within 2 to 3 days.*

Yield: $2^{1/2}$ cups

Endless summer salsa

2 dozen very ripe tomatoes, peeled, chopped
4 to 5 green bell peppers, chopped
3 to 4 medium onions, chopped
½ cup plus 1 tablespoon finely chopped jalapeño chiles
   (commercially prepared)
4 to 5 garlic cloves, chopped
2 (6-ounce) cans tomato paste
½ cup vinegar
¼ cup packed brown sugar
2 teaspoons pickling salt

- Cook the tomatoes over medium heat in a stockpot, simmering for 8 to 10 minutes.
- Drain and discard at least 1 quart of juice.
- Add the bell peppers, onions and jalapeño chiles.
- Mix in the garlic, tomato paste, vinegar, brown sugar and pickling salt.
- Cook over low heat for 20 to 25 minutes or until thickened.
- Spoon into hot, sterilized 1-pint jars, leaving ½ inch headspace; seal with 2-piece lids.
- Process in a boiling water bath for 20 minutes.

You may substitute 12 to 14 fresh jalapeño chiles, however, the ones that come chopped in a jar will save time. Prepared minced garlic is also a time saver.

For a different flavor, try using pickling spice rather than pickling salt. It gives an initial sweetness before the heat sets in.

Yield: 12 pints

Copper pennies

THIS IS A DELICIOUS AND COLORFUL DISH. PACKAGE IN A CLEAR
CONTAINER SO THE COLORS CAN SHOW THROUGH.

2 pounds carrots, peeled
Salt to taste
1 small green bell pepper, chopped
1 medium onion, thinly sliced
1 (15-ounce) can tomato soup
1/2 cup vegetable oil
1 cup sugar
3/4 cup white vinegar
1 teaspoon prepared mustard
1 teaspoon Worcestershire sauce

- Slice the carrots crosswise.
- Cook in salted water to cover in a saucepan until
  tender; drain.
- Layer the carrots, bell pepper and onion in a
  glass dish.
- Combine the soup, oil, sugar, vinegar, mustard
  and Worcestershire sauce in a bowl and mix well.
- Pour over the carrot mixture.
- Chill, tightly covered, for 8 to 10 hours before
  serving.

This side dish will keep well for 1 week.

Yield: 8 servings

Corn relish

PACKAGE THIS RELISH IN A CLEAR CONTAINER AND TIE WITH RAFFIA
FOR A COLORFUL GIFT.

$\frac{1}{2}$ cup cider vinegar
$\frac{1}{4}$ cup sugar
$\frac{1}{4}$ cup salt
$\frac{1}{4}$ teaspoon hot sauce
$\frac{1}{4}$ teaspoon celery seeds
$\frac{1}{4}$ teaspoon mustard seeds
1 (15-ounce) can whole kernel corn, drained
2 tablespoons chopped green bell pepper
2 tablespoons chopped pimento
1 tablespoon minced onion

- Combine the vinegar, sugar, salt, hot sauce, celery seeds and mustard seeds in a saucepan.
- Bring to a boil and cook for 2 minutes. Remove from the heat.
- Combine the corn, bell pepper, pimento, onion and vinegar mixture in a dish and mix well.
- Chill, covered, until serving time.
- Serve cold with a slotted spoon.

This relish keeps well in the refrigerator.

Yield: 6 to 8 servings

Marinated vegetable salad

THIS COLORFUL SALAD LOOKS GREAT PACKAGED IN CLEAR MASON
JARS TIED WITH RIBBON.

2 tomatoes, chopped
2 cucumbers, chopped
2 onions, sliced
2 (15-ounce) cans French-style green beans,
    drained
1 (8-ounce) bottle Italian salad dressing

- Combine the tomatoes, cucumbers, onions and
  green beans in a glass dish.
- Pour the dressing over the vegetables.
- Marinate, covered, in the refrigerator for 8 to
  10 hours before serving.

*You may peel the tomatoes and cucumbers
if desired.*

Yield: 12 to 16 servings

summer

Picnic slaw

1 large head cabbage, cored, chopped
1 green bell pepper, chopped
3 to 4 ribs celery, chopped
4 medium onions, chopped
1 (2-ounce) jar chopped pimentos
2 cups white vinegar
3½ cups sugar
1½ teaspoons celery seeds
1 teaspoon mustard seeds
1 teaspoon salt

- Combine the cabbage, bell pepper, celery, onions and pimentos in a large bowl and mix well. Set aside.
- Combine the vinegar, sugar, celery seeds, mustard seeds and salt in a large saucepan.
- Cook over medium heat until the sugar is dissolved, stirring constantly.
- Add the cabbage mixture to the dressing and simmer for 6 minutes.
- Cool rapidly using an ice water bath.
- Chill, covered, for 24 hours before serving.

This slaw will keep well in the refrigerator for 2 to 3 months.

Yield: 20 servings

Sicilian olives

PACKAGE THE OLIVES WITH FRESH PARMESAN CHEESE AND A LOAF
OF CRUSTY BREAD.

1 (16-ounce) jar low-sodium whole green olives
½ cup extra-virgin olive oil
¼ cup red wine vinegar
3 garlic cloves, finely chopped
1 tablespoon oregano

- Drain the juice from the olives, keeping the olives
  in the jar.
- Whisk together the olive oil and vinegar in a bowl.
- Add the garlic and oregano and mix well.
- Pour over the olives. Seal the jar with the
  tight-fitting lid.
- Let stand for several hours, shaking occasionally
  to distribute the marinade.
- Serve as an appetizer with freshly grated
  Parmesan cheese and crusty Italian bread.

*Try draining the marinade onto a bread plate
and topping with grated cheese for a tasty
bread dip.*

Yield: 8 servings

Sweet-and-hot dill pickles

1 (1-gallon) jar whole kosher dill pickles
7 cups sugar
2 ounces hot sauce

- Drain the pickles, discarding the juice.
- Slice the pickles into 1- to 2-inch chunks and return to the pickle jar.
- Add the sugar and hot sauce to the pickles.
- Seal the jar with the tight-fitting lid and shake until the sugar is dissolved.
- Let stand at room temperature for 13 days, shaking the jar 1 to 2 times per day.
- Chill the jar on day 14 until ready to serve. The pickles are now ready to enjoy.

You may substitute baby dill pickles or dill pickle slices for the whole pickles. You may adjust the amount of sugar and hot sauce according to your taste.

Yield: 1 gallon

summer

Honey barbecue sauce

PACKAGE THIS SAUCE IN A CLEAR CANNING JAR AND TIE WITH A BANDANA.

Prepared barbecue sauce
Dijon mustard
Honey

- Combine equal amounts of the barbecue sauce, mustard and honey in a bowl and mix until well blended.
- You may add more or less of certain ingredients according to your taste.
- Brush on chicken breasts or wings while grilling.
- Store in the refrigerator for several months.

This sauce is also great to use for basting ribs or as a dip for chicken tenders.

Yield: variable

Steak rub

PACKAGE THIS RUB IN A 4-OUNCE CANNING JAR. ADD A LABEL AND RIBBON AND YOU HAVE THE PERFECT GIFT FOR THE BBQ CHEF.

1 cup minus 2 tablespoons salt
¼ cup each sugar and MSG
½ cup pepper
½ teaspoon garlic powder
¼ teaspoon basil

- Combine the salt, sugar, MSG, pepper, garlic powder and basil in a bowl and mix well. Store in an airtight container.
- Use as a rub on steaks, roasts or your choice of meat. (A little of this rub will go a long way!)
- Let stand for 5 minutes and grill or cook until meat tests done.

Yield: 2 cups

Chick 'n' rib rub

¼ cup paprika
1 to 2 tablespoons dark brown sugar
1 tablespoon sugar
2 teaspoons cayenne pepper
1 to 2 teaspoons salt
¼ to ½ teaspoon celery salt
1 teaspoon freshly ground black pepper
1 teaspoon garlic powder

- Combine the paprika, brown sugar, sugar, cayenne pepper, salt, celery salt, black pepper and garlic powder in a sealable plastic bag or an airtight container.
- Shake to mix thoroughly.
- Store away from heat or light.

This recipe is easy to double or triple and will keep well for up to 6 months.

One-half cup rub is enough for 2 chickens or 2 racks of ribs.

Yield: ½ cup

Sourdough bread

PACKAGE THIS BREAD WITH HOMEMADE JAMS AND HONEY BUTTER.

Starter
1 envelope dry yeast
1/2 cup warm water
1 cup bread flour
1/2 cup warm water
2 tablespoons sugar
2 tablespoons dry potato flakes

Bread
1 1/2 cups vegetable oil
1/4 cup sugar
1 1/2 cups warm water
5 3/4 cups bread flour
1 tablespoon salt
Melted butter

- For the starter, dissolve the yeast in 1/2 cup warm water in a bowl.
- Combine the bread flour, 1/2 cup warm water, sugar and dry potato flakes in a separate bowl and mix until smooth.
- Add the yeast mixture and mix well.
- Let rise, covered, in a warm place for 1 hour.
- For the bread, combine the oil and sugar in a large bowl and mix well.
- Add the starter mixture and mix well.
- Stir in the warm water, bread flour and salt.
- Knead on a floured surface until smooth and elastic.
- Place in a greased bowl, turning to coat the surface.
- Let rise, covered, in a warm place for 4 hours.
- Divide into 3 portions. Knead each portion again.
- Place into 3 greased loaf pans. Brush the tops with oil.
- Let rise, covered, for 2 hours.
- Bake at 325 degrees for 20 minutes.
- Brush the tops with melted butter.
- Let cool before removing from the pans.

You may also bake this bread in miniature loaf pans for individual loaves. Although this is an all-day recipe, it is better than having to "feed" your starter every 3 days.

Yield: 3 loaves

Lemon pound cake

PACKAGE THIS CAKE WITH OTHER LEMON ITEMS SUCH AS LEMONADE, FRESH LEMONS, AND LEMON PUDDING FOR A REFRESHING LEMON-THEME GIFT.

2/3 cup water
1 (3-ounce) package lemon gelatin
1 (2-layer) package yellow cake mix
1/2 cup (1 stick) margarine, melted
4 eggs
Confectioners' sugar glaze

- Bring the water to a boil in a small saucepan.
- Stir in the gelatin until dissolved. Remove from the heat.
- Combine the cake mix and melted margarine in a mixing bowl.
- Beat at low speed until well blended.
- Add the eggs 1 at a time, beating well after each addition.
- Add the gelatin mixture and beat at medium speed for 2 minutes.
- Pour into a greased bundt pan.
- Bake at 325 degrees for 45 minutes.
- Turn off the oven and let the cake sit in the oven for 5 minutes or until the cake pulls away from the side of the pan.
- Remove from the oven and let the cake cool completely on a wire rack.
- Invert the cake onto a serving plate and drizzle with a confectioners' sugar glaze.

Try using the lemon-flavored confectioners' sugar and follow the directions on the back of the box for the glaze.

Yield: 16 servings

Orange blossoms

THESE DELICIOUS TREATS ARE WONDERFUL TO SERVE AT ANY KIND OF SHOWER OR TEA. AND THEY MAKE A WONDERFUL GIFT FOR THAT SOMEONE SPECIAL. THEY ARE SO EASY TO PREPARE IN ADVANCE, BUT PEOPLE WILL THINK YOU HAVE BEEN WORKING ALL DAY!

1 (2-layer) package yellow cake mix
2 (1-pound) packages confectioners' sugar
2/3 cup fresh lemon juice
1 1/3 cups orange juice

- Prepare the cake mix according to the package directions.
- Spoon the batter into greased miniature muffin tins.
- Bake according to the package directions for miniature muffin tins.
- Combine the confectioners' sugar, lemon juice and orange juice in a bowl and mix well until the confectioners' sugar is dissolved.
- Remove the muffins from the tins immediately.
- Dip the hot muffins in the sugar and juice mixture and place on waxed paper on a baking sheet.
- Chill until serving time. Serve cold.

The blossoms freeze well. Remove from the freezer 1 hour prior to serving.

Orange Blossoms are best when prepared in miniature muffin tins or muffin top tins. Standard size muffin tins are too large to allow the confectioners' sugar mixture to saturate the blossoms. You may need to reduce the cooking time for the muffin top tins and watch them closely to prevent them from getting too brown.

Yield: 12 to 15 servings

Blondies

½ cup (1 stick) butter, melted
2 cups packed brown sugar
2 eggs, beaten
1 teaspoon vanilla extract
1 cup pecans, chopped
1½ cups self-rising flour

- Combine the melted butter, brown sugar and eggs in a mixing bowl and beat until light and fluffy.
- Mix in the vanilla and pecans.
- Add the flour and beat until well mixed.
- Spread the mixture into a lightly greased 9×13-inch baking pan.
- Bake at 350 degrees for 25 minutes.
- Let cool before cutting into squares.

Yield: 2 dozen

summer

Chocolate nut crispies

½ cup sugar
½ cup light corn syrup
1 cup creamy peanut butter
1 tablespoon margarine
2½ cups crisp rice cereal
1 cup (6 ounces) chocolate chips, melted
¼ cup chopped peanuts

- Combine the sugar and corn syrup in a large saucepan.
- Cook over medium heat until the sugar dissolves, stirring constantly.
- Add the peanut butter and margarine.
- Cook until melted, stirring constantly.
- Stir in the cereal.
- Spread in a greased 9×13-inch glass dish.
- Spread the melted chocolate chips over the top.
- Sprinkle with the peanuts.
- Chill, covered, for 1 hour.
- Cut into bars to serve.

Yield: 2 dozen

Rock candy

1 piece of cotton string
1 pencil or stick
1 paper clip
1 glass jar
1 cup water
2 cups sugar
Food color of choice

- Tie a short piece of cotton string to the middle of the pencil or stick.
- Attach the paper clip to the end of the string for weight.
- Moisten the string and roll in a small amount of sugar to attract the crystals.
- Place the pencil over the top of the glass jar with the string hanging down inside.
- Heat the water to boiling in a saucepan and stir in the sugar until dissolved.
- Add a few drops of food color if desired.
- Pour into the prepared glass jar.
- Let stand for a couple days. Crystals should start forming within a few hours to a few days.
- Rock candy is done when the crystals stop forming.

To make the biggest crystals faster, heat the sugar water mixture a second time to boiling and dissolve as much additional sugar into it as possible. You may also use wooden skewers instead of string to make iced tea stirrers.

Yield: variable

Slow-cooker candy

2 pounds white chocolate
1 (4-ounce) bar German's sweet chocolate
3 cups (18 ounces) semisweet chocolate chips
24 ounces dry roasted peanuts

- Combine the white chocolate, German's sweet chocolate and semisweet chocolate chips in a slow cooker.
- Cook on Low for 2 hours; do not stir.
- Add the peanuts and stir to mix well.
- Drop by teaspoonfuls onto waxed paper. Let cool.
- Store in an airtight container.

You may use salted or unsalted peanuts in this recipe.

Yield: 100 pieces

summer

No-cook mint patties

¼ cup (½ stick) butter or margarine, softened
⅓ cup light corn syrup
2 teaspoons peppermint extract
½ teaspoon salt
1 (1-pound) package confectioners' sugar, sifted
3 drops red or green food color

- Combine the butter, corn syrup, peppermint extract and salt in a large bowl and mix until well blended.
- Add the confectioners' sugar and mix well until smooth.
- Divide the mixture into 3 portions.
- Knead 1 drop of food color into each portion.
- To make the mints, pinch off a small amount and shape into a ball.
- Place on waxed paper and flatten with the back of a spoon or a fork.
- Let stand for several hours to dry completely before serving.

You may substitute any flavoring extract according to taste.

Vary the color of the mints according to the holiday or event. These are great for showers, parties or even tailgating. Use your team's colors to give these mints added panache.

Yield: 6 dozen

Peanut butter pie

8 ounces cream cheese, softened
1 (14-ounce) can sweetened condensed milk
¾ cup creamy peanut butter
3 tablespoons lemon juice
1 teaspoon vanilla extract
4 ounces whipped topping
1 (9-inch) graham cracker pie shell

- Beat the cream cheese in a mixing bowl until light and fluffy.
- Add the sweetened condensed milk and peanut butter and beat until smooth.
- Stir in the lemon juice and vanilla.
- Fold in the whipped topping.
- Spoon into the pie shell.
- Chill, covered, for 4 hours or until set.

This pie will keep well for 1 week in the refrigerator.

Yield: 6 to 8 servings

summer

Cherry crunch

1 (16-ounce) can cherry pie filling
1 (2-layer) package yellow cake mix
½ cup (1 stick) butter or margarine, sliced
½ cup chopped pecans (optional)

- Pour the cherry pie filling in the bottom of an 8×8-inch baking pan.
- Sprinkle the cake mix on top, covering the filling completely. (You may not want to use all of the cake mix.)
- Dot with the butter.
- Sprinkle the top with pecans if desired.
- Bake at 350 degrees for 35 to 40 minutes.

Yield: 8 servings

summer

Chocolate fondue

PACKAGE THIS DELICIOUS TREAT WITH A POUND CAKE AND
KABOB SKEWERS.

1 cup chocolate-flavored sweetened
    condensed milk
1/4 cup half-and-half

- Combine the sweetened condensed milk and
  half-and-half in a bowl and mix until well blended.
- Chill, covered, until serving time.
- Serve with fresh fruit or pound cake cubes
  on kabobs.

*You may heat in the microwave until of desired
temperature.*

Yield: 1 1/4 cups

autumn

*A*s summer fades into autumn, life is about winding down. Autumn is the time to breathe, sigh, and relax. It is back to school, football, parties and fellowship, not to mention Columbus Day, Halloween, and Thanksgiving. It is time to open the windows and enjoy the fresh autumn breeze after suffering through the hot and humid days of summer.

Autumn is the season for friendship gifts. It is margarita balls for tailgating, caramel corn for Halloween, and pecan pie for Thanksgiving. It is candied pecans and a movie, herb vinegars with the last greens from the garden, and haystacks for school lunches. Autumn is comfort. The comfort of friends and the comfort of food. It is quiet nights and Saturday games. It is the comfort of togetherness.

Contents

Ugly dip

THIS DIP MAY LOOK UGLY, BUT THERE IS NOTHING UGLY ABOUT THE TASTE. TAKE IT TO A TAILGATING PARTY AND LISTEN TO YOUR FRIENDS RAVE.

1 (14-ounce) can stewed tomatoes
1 cup mild picante sauce
1 cup hot picante sauce
1 (4-ounce) can sliced black olives, drained
1 bunch green onions, finely chopped
1 tablespoon garlic salt
1 tablespoon white vinegar
1 tablespoon vegetable oil

- Pour the stewed tomatoes into a blender container.
- Process until the tomatoes are chopped, but not puréed.
- Combine the tomatoes, picante sauces, black olives and green onions in a bowl and mix well.
- Add the garlic salt, vinegar and oil and mix well.
- Chill, covered, until serving time.

The dip will be too thin if you process the tomatoes too long. For a thicker dip, do not add all the tomatoes.

Yield: 4 cups (30 servings)

Trail mix

ATTACH A BAG OF THIS MIX TO A NATURE BOOK FOR THE PERFECT
GIFT TO GIVE TO ANY OUTDOORS LOVER YOU KNOW.

1 cup "M & M's" Chocolate Candies
1 cup mixed nuts
½ cup raisins

- Combine the chocolate candies, nuts and raisins
  in a bowl and mix well.
- Store in an airtight container.

*You may vary the amount of ingredients according
to taste or for the amount of Trail Mix you need
to make.*

*For a variation, try adding different types of dried
fruit or goldfish crackers.*

Yield: 2½ cups

autumn

Barbecue sauce

½ cup pineapple juice
½ cup ketchup
⅓ cup vinegar
¼ cup vegetable oil
¼ cup Worcestershire sauce
¼ cup hot sauce
¼ cup chopped onion
3 tablespoons brown sugar
1 teaspoon chili powder
⅛ teaspoon salt (optional)

- Combine the pineapple juice, ketchup, vinegar, oil, Worcestershire sauce, hot sauce, onion, brown sugar, chili powder and salt in a large saucepan and mix well.
- Bring to a boil over medium-high heat and reduce the heat. Simmer until the desired consistency is reached, stirring frequently.
- Remove from the heat and let cool. Store in an airtight container in the refrigerator.

This sauce will keep well for several weeks in the refrigerator.

This Barbecue Sauce is great to use as a baste when grilling chicken or ribs. It is also good as a dipping sauce for chicken tenders or meatballs.

Yield: 2¼ cups

Marinara sauce

PACKAGE THIS SAUCE WITH A BAG OF FRESH, SOFT BREADSTICKS.

1 (15-ounce) can tomato sauce
1/2 teaspoon salt
1/4 teaspoon pepper
1/4 teaspoon garlic powder
1/4 teaspoon basil
1/4 teaspoon oregano
1/4 teaspoon thyme

- Combine the tomato sauce, salt, pepper, garlic powder, basil, oregano and thyme in a saucepan and mix well.
- Cook over medium heat until mixture simmers and is heated through.
- Remove from the heat and let cool completely.
- Store in an airtight container in the refrigerator.
- The sauce will keep for 3 to 4 weeks.
- Let the sauce come to room temperature or heat in a saucepan on the stove before serving.

Yield: 1 1/2 cups

autumn

Alfredo sauce

PACKAGE THIS SAUCE WITH NOODLES AND FRESH BREADSTICKS AS A GIFT FOR PASTA LOVERS.

3/4 cup ranch salad dressing
1/2 cup sour cream
1/4 cup grated Parmesan cheese

- Combine the salad dressing, sour cream and cheese in a bowl and mix well.
- Chill, covered, for 4 to 12 hours before serving.
- To serve, heat in a saucepan on the stove or in a microwave-safe container in the microwave. Use as a dip for warm, fresh breadsticks or serve over hot buttered noodles.

Yield: 1 1/2 cups

Sweet-and-sour sauce

1 (8-ounce) bottle Russian or Catalina salad dressing
1 envelope Lipton onion soup mix
1 (8-ounce) jar apricot preserves

- Combine the salad dressing, soup mix and preserves in a bowl and mix well.
- Chill, covered, until ready to use.
- To serve, use to baste chicken. Pour over chicken breasts in a baking dish. Bake, uncovered, at 350 degrees for 1 hour or until chicken tests done, basting occasionally.

You may also pour over chicken wings in a slow cooker. Cook on Low until wings are done.

Yield: 2 1/4 cups

Horseradish mustard

½ cup sweet hot mustard
2 teaspoons prepared horseradish
⅛ teaspoon garlic salt
⅛ teaspoon cayenne pepper

- Combine the mustard, horseradish, garlic salt and cayenne pepper in a bowl and mix well.
- Chill, covered, for 8 to 10 hours to allow the flavors to blend.
- Serve with roast beef and prime rib.
- Store in an airtight container in the refrigerator.

Yield: ½ cup

autumn

Baking mix

PACKAGE THIS MIX WITH SOME OF YOUR FAVORITE BAKING RECIPES AS A GIFT FOR THE COOK YOU KNOW.

8 cups flour
1 1/4 cups nonfat dry milk powder
1/4 cup baking powder
1 tablespoon salt
2 cups shortening

- Combine the flour, milk powder, baking powder and salt in a large bowl and mix well.
- Cut in the shortening with a pastry blender or 2 knives until the mixture is crumbly.

Use this in place of commercial baking mix.

Yield: 10 cups

Honey butter

PACKAGE THIS BUTTER WITH BISCUIT MIX FOR A DELICIOUS GIFT.

1/2 cup (1 stick) unsalted butter, softened
1/2 cup honey

- Combine the butter and honey in a blender container.
- Process at low speed until well blended.
- Spoon into an airtight container.
- Chill until serving time.

Yield: 1 1/4 cups

Sour cream rolls

PACKAGE THESE ROLLS IN A BASKET AND TIE UP WITH PRETTY DISH TOWELS.

   1 cup sour cream
   ½ cup (1 stick) butter or margarine, melted
   1 cup self-rising flour

- Combine the sour cream, melted butter and flour in a bowl and mix well.
- Spoon into greased muffin tins or miniature muffin tins.
- Bake at 450 degrees for 15 minutes.
- Serve with your favorite soup or as a snack with drinks. Leftover rolls are great.

   Yield: 1 to 3 dozen (depending on the muffin tin size)

autumn

Caramel bubble rolls

PRESENT THE ROLLS IN A COVERED 9×13-INCH PAN TIED UP WITH A RIBBON. IF PREPARED IN A BUNDT PAN, INVERT ONTO A PRETTY PLATE AND WRAP WITH COLORED PLASTIC WRAP.

2 loaves frozen bread dough
1/2 cup (1 stick) butter or margarine
1 cup packed brown sugar
1 (4-ounce) package vanilla cook-and-serve pudding mix
2 tablespoons milk
1 1/2 teaspoons cinnamon (optional)

- Thaw the bread in the refrigerator for 8 to 10 hours; do not let rise.
- Melt the butter in a saucepan. Add the brown sugar, pudding mix, milk and cinnamon and bring to a boil, stirring constantly.
- Remove from the heat and keep warm to avoid mixture getting too thick.
- Tear 1 loaf of bread dough into small pieces and arrange over the bottom of a greased 9×13-inch pan.
- Pour half of the butter mixture over the bread dough.
- Tear the other loaf of bread dough into small pieces and place on top.
- Pour the remaining butter mixture over the bread dough.
- Let rise for 1 hour.
- Bake at 350 degrees for 30 minutes.

You may also prepare these rolls by layering the bread dough and butter mixture in a bundt pan. If prepared in a bundt pan, serve by letting guests pull apart the "bubbles" of bread.

Yield: 15 servings

Pumpkin roll

3 eggs
1 cup sugar
2/3 cup canned pumpkin
1 tablespoon lemon juice
3/4 cup flour
1 tablespoon baking powder

1 teaspoon cinnamon
1/2 teaspoon nutmeg
1/2 teaspoon salt
1 cup chopped pecans
Confectioners' sugar
Cream Cheese Filling

- Beat the eggs in a large mixing bowl at high speed for 4 minutes.
- Add the sugar and beat at high speed for 1 minute.
- Add the pumpkin and lemon juice and beat well.
- Mix the flour, baking powder, cinnamon, nutmeg and salt together.
- Add the flour mixture to the pumpkin mixture gradually, mixing well.
- Grease a 10×15-inch baking pan and line with waxed paper.
- Pour the mixture into the prepared pan and sprinkle with the pecans.
- Bake at 375 degrees for 15 minutes.
- Invert onto a clean kitchen towel that has been dusted with confectioners' sugar.
- Roll the warm cake in the towel lengthwise, as for a jelly roll.
- Let cool on a wire rack for at least 2 hours.
- Unroll the cooled cake and carefully remove the towel. Spread the Cream Cheese Filling to the edge and reroll. Place seam side down on a serving plate.

The roll may be frozen for several months. Thaw before serving.

Yield: 8 to 10 servings

Cream cheese filling

8 ounces cream cheese, softened
1 cup confectioners' sugar

1 teaspoon vanilla extract

- Combine the cream cheese, confectioners' sugar and vanilla in a mixing bowl.
- Beat until well blended and of spreading consistency.

Funnel cakes

PACKAGE THE FLOUR AND SUGAR MIX WITH A FUNNEL AND RECIPE INSTRUCTIONS ON THE GIFT TAG.

2½ cups self-rising flour
¼ cup sugar
1⅓ cups milk
2 eggs, lightly beaten
Vegetable oil
Confectioners' sugar

- Combine the flour and sugar in a bowl and mix well.
- Add the milk and eggs and mix until well blended.
- Pour the oil into a heavy skillet to ¼ inch deep.
- Heat the oil to 375 degrees.
- Cover the bottom of a funnel with your finger.
- Pour ¼ cup of the batter into the funnel.
- Hold the funnel over the skillet, remove your finger and release the batter into the hot oil in a circular motion.
- Cook until golden brown.
- Remove the funnel cake with a spatula and drain on paper towels.
- Sprinkle with desired amount of confectioners' sugar.

Yield: 8 servings

autumn

Cake mix oatmeal cookies

PACKAGE THESE COOKIES IN A RESEALABLE CONTAINER WHICH IS JUST AS MUCH A GIFT AS THE COOKIES. ADD A PERSONAL TOUCH BY DRAWING DESIGNS ON IT.

1 (2-layer) package chocolate cake mix
2 cups quick-cooking oats
1 cup sugar
2 eggs
1 cup vegetable oil
1 cup chopped pecans
1½ teaspoons almond extract

- Combine the cake mix, oats and sugar in a large bowl and mix well.
- Beat the eggs and oil in a mixing bowl.
- Add to the dry ingredients and mix well.
- Stir in the pecans and almond extract.
- Drop by rounded teaspoonfuls onto a cookie sheet.
- Bake at 350 degrees for 12 minutes.
- Store in an airtight container.

You may substitute yellow cake mix for the chocolate and vanilla extract for the almond.

Yield: 5 dozen

Peanut cookie bars

To GIVE AS A GIFT WITHOUT MAKING THE BARS, PACKAGE ALL THE INGREDIENTS (EXCEPT MARGARINE) IN A PRETTY BAKING PAN WITH A WOODEN SPOON.

½ cup (1 stick) margarine
1½ cups graham cracker crumbs
1 (14-ounce) can sweetened condensed milk
2 cups (12 ounces) peanut butter chips
1 cup (6 ounces) semisweet chocolate chips
1 cup chopped Spanish peanuts

- Preheat the oven to 350 degrees.
- Melt the margarine in a 9×13-inch baking dish in the oven.
- Remove from the oven and stir in the graham cracker crumbs.
- Press evenly into the bottom of the prepared dish to form a crust.
- Pour the sweetened condensed milk evenly over the crust.
- Sprinkle with the peanut butter chips, chocolate chips and top with the peanuts.
- Bake at 350 degrees for 25 minutes or until the edges are golden brown.
- Chill for at least 1 hour before cutting into bars to serve.

Yield: 3 dozen

autumn

Potato chip cookies

A unique ingredient adds a little panache to a basic recipe. Package these cookies in clear plastic wrap and place in an empty potato chip bag for gift giving.

1 cup (2 sticks) margarine, softened
1/2 cup sugar
1 teaspoon vanilla extract
1/2 cup chopped pecans
1/2 cup crushed potato chips
2 cups flour
Sugar

- Cream the margarine and 1/2 cup sugar in a mixing bowl until light and fluffy.
- Add the vanilla, pecans, potato chips and flour and mix well.
- Shape into tablespoon-size balls.
- Flatten with the bottom of a glass and dip in sugar.
- Place on a cookie sheet.
- Bake at 350 degrees for 15 minutes or until light brown.

Yield: 3 dozen

autumn

Margarita balls

THESE TREATS ARE BEST WHEN ALLOWED TO CHILL THOROUGHLY. IF YOU CAN WAIT THAT LONG!

1 (12-ounce) package vanilla wafers
1 cup (8 ounces) blanched sliced almonds
1/4 cup tequila
1/4 cup orange marmalade
2 tablespoons lime juice
2 tablespoons light corn syrup
4 ounces white chocolate, melted
Sugar

- Crumble the vanilla wafers into a blender container.
- Add the almonds and process until the consistency of fine crumbs.
- Spoon into a large bowl.
- Combine the tequila, orange marmalade, lime juice and corn syrup in a blender container.
- Process until smooth.
- Add the melted white chocolate to the blender container and process until just mixed.
- Pour the tequila mixture over the crumb mixture and mix well.
- Shape into 1-inch balls.
- Roll in sugar to coat well.
- Store in an airtight container in the refrigerator.

Yield: 3 dozen

Caramel corn

THIS DELICIOUS SNACK WILL STAY FRESH IN THE FREEZER INDEFINITELY.

1 cup (2 sticks) margarine, softened
1/2 cup light corn syrup
2 cups packed brown sugar
1/4 teaspoon cream of tartar
1/4 teaspoon baking soda
6 quarts popped popcorn

- Combine the margarine, corn syrup, brown sugar, cream of tartar and baking soda in a large saucepan.
- Bring to a boil and boil for 5 minutes until the sugar dissolves, stirring constantly.
- Pour over the popped corn in a large bowl or roasting pan and mix to coat well.
- Pour onto baking sheets.
- Bake at 200 degrees for 1 hour, stirring occasionally.
- Store in sealable plastic bags.

Yield: 6 quarts

Candied pecans

1 egg white
1 teaspoon cold water
1 pound pecan halves
1 cup sugar
1 teaspoon cinnamon

- Beat the egg white and water in a mixing bowl until frothy.
- Add the pecans and stir to coat well.
- Combine the sugar and cinnamon in a small bowl and stir into the pecans.
- Spread the pecans onto a baking sheet.
- Bake at 275 degrees for 1 hour, stirring occasionally.
- Store in an airtight container.

Yield: 1 pound

autumn

Haystacks

KEEPING WITH THE AGRICULTURAL THEME OF THESE CLUSTERS, PACKAGE THEM IN A CAP PURCHASED AT YOUR LOCAL CO-OP OR IMPLEMENT DEALER. WRAP THEM IN CLEAR CELLOPHANE, TIE WITH A BOW, AND PLACE IN THE CAP.

2 cups (12 ounces) butterscotch chips
1 (14-ounce) can sweetened condensed milk
1 (6-ounce) can chow mein noodles
1 cup dry roasted peanuts

- Combine the butterscotch chips and sweetened condensed milk in a heavy saucepan.
- Cook over low heat until the butterscotch chips are melted, stirring occasionally.
- Combine the chow mein noodles and peanuts in a large bowl and mix well.
- Pour the butterscotch mixture over the chow mein noodles and peanuts.
- Stir to coat well.
- Drop by spoonfuls onto waxed paper-lined baking sheets.
- Chill for 2 hours or until firm.

You may substitute chocolate chips for the butterscotch chips.

Yield: 2 to 4 dozen

Peanut butter cornflake treats

PACKAGE THIS SNACK IN SMALL TREAT BAGS FOR PARTY FAVORS OR
HALLOWEEN GIFTS.

  1 cup sugar
  1 cup light corn syrup
  1½ cups creamy peanut butter
  4 cups cornflakes

- Combine the sugar and corn syrup in a saucepan.
- Bring to a boil and boil until the sugar dissolves,
  stirring constantly.
- Add the peanut butter and cook until it melts,
  stirring constantly.
- Add the cornflakes and mix gently.
- Drop by spoonfuls onto waxed paper.
- Let cool until firm.

You may also use crunchy peanut butter if desired.

Yield: 3 dozen

autumn

Peanut butter fudge

FUDGE MAKES A GREAT GIFT THAT EVERYONE LOVES. COVER WITH CLEAR OR COLORED PLASTIC WRAP AND TIE WITH A BOW.

2 cups sugar
1/2 cup milk
1 1/3 cups creamy peanut butter
1 (7-ounce) jar marshmallow creme

- Combine the sugar and milk in a saucepan.
- Bring to a boil and boil for 3 minutes or until the sugar dissolves, stirring constantly.
- Add the peanut butter and marshmallow creme and cook until melted, stirring constantly.
- Pour quickly into a greased 8-inch square pan.
- Chill, covered, until firm.
- Cut into squares to serve.

You may also use crunchy peanut butter if desired.

Yield: 3 to 4 dozen

autumn

Pecan pie

FOR A BEAUTIFUL PRESENTATION, PLACE THE PIE ON TOP OF WHOLE PECANS IN THE SHELL IN A PRETTY BASKET. TIE A BOW ON THE BASKET AND IT IS READY FOR GIVING.

5 eggs
1 cup sugar
1 1/2 cups light corn syrup
6 tablespoons butter, melted
1 1/2 teaspoons vanilla extract
1/2 teaspoon salt
1 1/2 cups chopped pecans
2 unbaked (9-inch) pie shells

- Beat the eggs and sugar in a mixing bowl until thick and pale yellow.
- Add the corn syrup, melted butter, vanilla and salt and beat until well blended.
- Stir in the pecans.
- Pour into the pie shells.
- Bake at 350 degrees for 40 to 50 minutes or until set.
- Let cool on a wire rack.

These pies freeze well.

Yield: 16 servings

Eclairs

2 (4-ounce) packages vanilla instant pudding mix
2⅔ cups milk
8 ounces whipped topping
1 (16-ounce) container prepared chocolate
    frosting
1 (16-ounce) package graham crackers

- Mix the pudding mix and milk in a bowl according to the package directions.
- Chill, covered, for 5 minutes or until just set.
- Add the whipped topping to the prepared pudding and mix well.
- Melt the chocolate frosting in a microwave-safe container in the microwave until pourable.
- Layer the graham crackers and pudding in a 9×13-inch dish.
- Pour the chocolate frosting over the top.
- Chill, covered, for 8 to 10 hours before serving.

You may use any variety of prepared chocolate frosting such as dark or milk chocolate.

Yield: 15 servings

autumn

Herb vinegar

TIE SEVERAL SPRIGS OF THE FRESH HERB OF CHOICE TO THE BOTTLE OR JAR FOR A PRETTY PRESENTATION.

Fresh herbs such as: basil, dill, mint, oregano, parsley, rosemary and thyme
1 gallon white vinegar

- Fill a plastic gallon jug half full with the fresh herb of choice.
- Heat the vinegar in a saucepan until very hot; do not boil.
- Pour over the herbs to fill the container. (You may use a funnel to make the pouring easier.) Seal tightly.
- Store in a dark, cool place for 4 to 6 weeks, shaking the contents daily.
- Strain into decorative bottles and jars. Use plastic or cork tops to seal the containers. Do not use metal tops.

You may experiment using various herbs or fruit to make your own special flavored vinegar.

Yield: 1 gallon

Colored sugar

ADD A FESTIVE TOUCH TO YOUR TAILGATING. COLOR THE SUGAR OR SALT THE COLORS OF YOUR FAVORITE TEAMS.

1 cup sugar
4 to 6 drops food color

- Combine the sugar and enough of the food color of choice in a bowl and mix well until the color is blended. Let dry.
- Stir to break up any sugar lumps.
- Store in an airtight container.

You may substitute salt for the sugar. Use the sugar as a dip for fresh fruit or use the salt to coat the rims of Margarita glasses.

Yield: 1 cup

winter

Winter is a time of both rest and celebration. It is staying warm inside yet still enjoying the chill outside. It is Christmas, New Year's, and Valentine's as well as the Super Bowl and collegiate play-offs. It is sledding and card parties.

Winter celebrations bring forth the chef in all of us. It is sand art brownies, peanut brittle, and coffeecino for the gourmand. It is grog, cider, and spiced tea for sipping with its holiday scent to tantalize our noses. Winter is also the season for aches and ailments. Ward off the chills and ills with five-can slow-cooker soup, wild rice soup, or a winter favorite—chili.

Winter is planning ahead. It is preparing hummingbird cake, cheese balls, and buckeyes to avoid the seasonal rush. Winter is about variety. From holidays and celebrations to sports and indoor entertainment, winter is definitely about the variety of celebrations.

Contents

The recipe (sparkling punch)

THIS IS THE PERFECT HOSTESS GIFT. PACKAGE BOTTLES OF GRAPE JUICE AND GINGER ALE IN A PRETTY BASKET WITH CHAMPAGNE FLUTES FOR A NEW YEAR'S EVE GATHERING.

White grape juice
Ginger ale

- Combine equal parts white grape juice and ginger ale in a large container.
- Serve over ice.

Yield: variable

Grog

1 (64-ounce) bottle apple juice
1 (64-ounce) bottle cranberry juice
1 (12-ounce) can frozen orange juice concentrate, thawed
½ cup water
3 cinnamon sticks
12 whole cloves
Whiskey (optional)

- Combine the apple juice, cranberry juice, orange juice concentrate, water, cinnamon sticks and cloves in a large stockpot.
- Heat until the desired temperature is reached.
- Strain to remove the cinnamon sticks and cloves before serving.
- You may serve this beverage hot or cold. Add ½ shot of whiskey to each serving if desired.

Yield: 5 quarts (30 servings)

Hot spiced cider

PACKAGE THIS CIDER WITH INSULATED MUGS AND CINNAMON STICKS
TO BE USED AS STIRRERS.

4 cups apple cider
2/3 cup packed brown sugar
2 cinnamon sticks
4 to 8 whole cloves
1/4 teaspoon nutmeg
1/4 teaspoon ginger

- Combine the apple cider, brown sugar, cinnamon
  sticks, cloves, nutmeg and ginger in a saucepan.
- Bring to a boil over high heat, stirring constantly.
- Reduce the heat to low.
- Simmer for 10 minutes.
- Strain to remove cinnamon sticks and cloves
  before serving.
- Store leftover cider in the refrigerator.

Yield: 8 servings

Hot cocoa mix

PACKAGE THIS MIX IN SEALABLE PLASTIC BAGS AND INSERT IN
DECORATED BROWN PAPER BAGS TIED WITH RIBBON.

1 (16-ounce) jar nondairy coffee creamer
1 (16-ounce) package chocolate instant drink mix
1 (1-pound) package confectioners' sugar
1 (8-ounce) package nonfat dry milk powder
10 tablespoons baking cocoa

- Combine the coffee creamer, chocolate instant
  drink mix, confectioners' sugar, dry milk powder
  and baking cocoa in a large bowl and mix well.
- Store in an airtight container.

To prepare Hot Cocoa:
- Combine 1/3 cup Hot Cocoa Mix and 1 cup hot
  water in a mug and mix well.

Yield: 7 cups

winter

Mint coffeecino

PACKAGE THE MINT COFFEECINO MIX IN SEALABLE PLASTIC BAGS WITH A MUG AND SEVERAL PEPPERMINT CANDY STICKS TO BE USED AS STIRRERS.

1/3 cup nondairy coffee creamer
1/4 to 1/3 cup sugar
1/4 cup instant coffee granules
2 tablespoons baking cocoa
8 peppermint candy disks, crushed

- Combine the coffee creamer, sugar, coffee granules, baking cocoa and crushed peppermint candy in a blender container.
- Process until all ingredients are well blended.
- Store the mix in an airtight container.

To prepare Mint Coffeecino:
- Combine 2 to 2 1/2 teaspoons of the Mint Coffeecino mix and 1 cup boiling water in a mug and mix well.

Crush the peppermint candy disks as much as possible before putting into the blender.

Yield: 1 cup

Mocha mix

1 cup chocolate instant drink mix
3/4 to 1 cup nondairy coffee creamer
1/3 to 2/3 cup instant coffee granules
1/2 cup sugar
1/2 teaspoon cinnamon
1/4 teaspoon nutmeg

- Combine the chocolate instant drink mix, coffee creamer, coffee granules, sugar, cinnamon and nutmeg in a bowl and mix well.
- Store in an airtight container.

To prepare Mocha:
- Combine 4 to 6 teaspoons of the Mocha Mix and 3/4 cup boiling water in a mug and mix well.

Yield: 3 cups

winter

Spiced tea

PRESENT THIS TEA IN AN INSULATED THERMOS. TIE WITH RAFFIA AND INSERT CINNAMON STICKS INTO THE BOW.

3 cinnamon sticks
14 whole cloves
4 family-size tea bags
2 cups boiling water
1 (4-ounce) package cherry gelatin
1 cup sugar
¼ cup lemon juice
1 (40-ounce) can pineapple juice
Water

- Combine the cinnamon sticks, cloves and tea bags in a bowl.
- Pour 2 cups boiling water in the bowl and let steep for 10 minutes.
- Strain into a 1-gallon stockpot.
- Add the gelatin and sugar and mix well.
- Add the lemon juice, pineapple juice and enough water to fill the container.
- Heat to the desired serving temperature and stir to mix well before serving.

Do not refrigerate or gelatin will set up.

Yield: 1 gallon (16 servings)

winter

Cheese balls

PACKAGE THIS APPETIZER WITH A PRETTY CHEESE PLATE AND KNIFE.

1 1/2 pounds American cheese, shredded
1 1/2 pounds sharp Cheddar cheese, shredded
1 1/2 pounds medium Cheddar cheese, shredded
1 pound mild Cheddar cheese, shredded
8 ounces cream cheese, softened
1 1/2 cups very finely chopped pecans
2 garlic cloves, minced
2 (4-ounce) jars chopped pimentos, mashed
3 tablespoons lemon juice
1/4 cup prepared mustard
1 tablespoon sugar
Red pepper or black pepper to taste
1 cup (or more) mayonnaise
Paprika
Chopped pecans

- Combine the American cheese, Cheddar cheese, cream cheese, 1 1/2 cups pecans, garlic, pimentos, lemon juice, mustard, sugar, red pepper and mayonnaise in a large bowl and mix well.
- Shape into small balls or logs.
- Roll the balls or logs in paprika and/or pecans to coat.
- Wrap in waxed paper and then wrap in foil.
- Chill until serving time.
- Serve with assorted crackers.

May also be frozen.

Yield: 14 cheese balls or logs

Ranch-style crackers

1 (14-ounce) package cheese crackers
1 envelope ranch salad dressing mix
1 to 1 1/8 teaspoons dillweed
1/4 cup vegetable oil
1/8 teaspoon lemon pepper (optional)
1/8 teaspoon seasoning salt (optional)

- Pour crackers into a 1-gallon resealable container or bag.
- Combine the dressing mix, dillweed, oil, lemon pepper and seasoning salt and mix well.
- Pour over the crackers and seal the container tightly.
- Shake until the crackers are well coated.
- Spread on a baking sheet.
- Bake at 250 degrees for 15 to 20 minutes, stirring once.

You may substitute oyster crackers or your favorite snack cracker for the cheese crackers.

Yield: 3 cups

Sausage balls

1 pound hot sausage, crumbled
2 cups shredded Cheddar cheese
3 cups baking mix

- Combine the sausage and cheese in a large bowl and mix well.
- Add the baking mix ½ cup at a time and mix well.
- Shape into balls.
- Place on a baking sheet.
- Bake at 350 degrees for 10 minutes or until brown. Let cool.
- Store in an airtight container in the refrigerator or may freeze.
- To prepare frozen sausage balls, heat in a microwave or conventional oven.

For a variation, try adding 8 ounces of finely chopped dates to the mixture before shaping into balls.

Yield: 4 dozen

Chili seasoning

PACKAGE THE DRY AND LIQUID INGREDIENTS SEPARATELY FOR GIFT GIVING. INCLUDE THE SPICES IN A DUTCH OVEN WITH THE INSTRUCTIONS ON THE GIFT TAG.

Chili ingredients:
1 to 1½ pounds ground beef
1 quart tomato juice
1 to 2 (15-ounce) cans kidney beans
2 tablespoons finely chopped jalapeño chiles, or ¾ cup salsa

Dry ingredients:
1 to 1½ teaspoons chili powder
¼ teaspoon pepper
⅛ teaspoon salt

Liquid ingredients:
3 tablespoons prepared mustard
2 tablespoons vinegar
1 teaspoon minced garlic

- Brown the ground beef in a skillet, stirring until the ground beef is crumbly; drain.
- Combine the ground beef, tomato juice, kidney beans and jalapeño chiles in a large stockpot. Stir in the dry ingredients. Add the liquid ingredients and mix well.
- Cook on low for 1 hour.

May also cook in a slow cooker on Low for 8 hours.

This chili freezes well. If doubling the recipe, do not double the jalapeño chiles, unless you prefer a hotter chili.

Yield: 6 to 8 servings

Five-can slow-cooker soup

PACKAGE ALL 5 CANS AND PREPARED MIXES IN A LARGE BROWN PAPER BAG THAT HAS BEEN DECORATED ESPECIALLY FOR YOUR RECIPIENT. SECURE WITH A BOW AND A GIFT TAG WITH THE RECIPE INSTRUCTIONS.

1 pound ground beef
1 large onion, chopped
1 (15-ounce) can pinto beans
1 (15-ounce) can ranch-style beans
1 (15-ounce) can tomatoes with green chiles
1 (15-ounce) can stewed tomatoes
1 (15-ounce) can corn (whole kernel or cream-style)
1 envelope ranch salad dressing mix
1 envelope taco seasoning mix
2 tablespoons chopped fresh cilantro (optional)

- Brown the ground beef with the onion in a skillet, stirring until the ground beef is crumbly; drain.
- Spoon into the slow cooker.
- Add the pinto beans, ranch-style beans, tomatoes with green chiles, stewed tomatoes, corn, ranch salad dressing mix, taco seasoning mix and cilantro and mix well.
- Cook on Low for 8 to 10 hours.
- Ladle into bowls to serve.
- Serve with corn bread and a green salad.

Yield: 6 to 8 servings

winter

Taco soup

This is a great soup to take to someone on a chilly winter day.

2 pounds ground beef
1 onion, chopped
1 envelope taco seasoning mix
1 envelope ranch salad dressing mix
1 (15-ounce) can chopped tomatoes
1 (15-ounce) can chopped tomatoes with green chiles
1 (15-ounce) can pinto beans
1 (15-ounce) can kidney beans
1 (15-ounce) can black beans
1 (15-ounce) can Shoe Peg corn

- Brown the ground beef with the onion in a skillet, stirring until the ground beef is crumbly; drain.
- Stir in the taco seasoning mix and ranch salad dressing mix.
- Spoon into a stockpot or Dutch oven.
- Add the tomatoes, tomatoes with green chiles, pinto beans, kidney beans, black beans and Shoe Peg corn and mix well.
- Simmer for 1 hour and 30 minutes.
- Ladle into bowls and top with shredded cheese, sour cream and corn chips.

Yield: 10 to 12 servings

Wild rice soup

PACKAGE THIS SOUP WITH A LOAF OF SOURDOUGH BREAD FOR A COMFORTING WINTER GIFT.

2 tablespoons butter
1 tablespoon minced onion
1/4 cup flour
4 cups chicken broth
2 cups cooked wild rice
1/2 teaspoon salt
1 cup half-and-half
2 tablespoons dry sherry (optional)

- Melt the butter in a saucepan over low heat.
- Add the onion and sauté until tender.
- Stir in the flour and add the broth gradually.
- Cook until thickened slightly, stirring constantly.
- Stir in the rice and salt and simmer for 5 minutes.
- Add the half-and-half and sherry and mix well.
- Let simmer on low until thoroughly heated through.
- Ladle into bowls to serve.

For a variation, you may also add finely chopped ham, grated carrots or slivered almonds.

This soup freezes well.

Yield: 6 servings

Jambalaya mix

PACKAGE THIS MIX WITH A LOAF OF HEARTY BREAD, SALAD GREENS, AND FRUIT FOR A COMPLETE MEAL. INCLUDE THE PREPARATION INSTRUCTIONS FOR THE JAMBALAYA.

Mix:
1 cup uncooked rice
1 to 2 tablespoons minced onion
1 tablespoon green pepper flakes
1 bay leaf
2 teaspoons beef bouillon granules
1/2 teaspoon garlic powder
1/2 teaspoon black pepper
1/4 teaspoon thyme
1/8 to 1/4 teaspoon crushed red pepper
1/2 teaspoon oregano (optional)
1/2 teaspoon basil (optional)

Main ingredients:
3 cups water
1 (8-ounce) can tomato sauce
1 cup chopped cooked chicken

• Combine the rice, minced onion, green pepper flakes, bay leaf, beef bouillon granules, garlic powder, black pepper, thyme, red pepper, oregano and basil and mix well.
• Store in an airtight container.

Yield: 1 1/2 cups mix

To prepare Jambalaya:
• Combine the mix, water and tomato sauce in a Dutch oven. Bring to a boil.
• Stir in the chicken and reduce the heat. Simmer for 20 to 25 minutes or until the rice is cooked.
• Remove the bay leaf before serving.

Yield: 8 servings

Corn bread mix

PACKAGE THE DRY INGREDIENTS IN A CLEAR SEALABLE PLASTIC BAG. TIE UP IN A BROWN PAPER BAG AND INCLUDE THE PREPARATION INSTRUCTIONS FOR THE CORN BREAD. GIVE AS A GIFT WITH A SMALL CAST-IRON SKILLET AND A WOODEN SPOON.

1½ cups self-rising cornmeal
1 tablespoon sugar

- Combine the cornmeal and sugar in a bowl and mix well.

To prepare Corn Bread:
- Combine the mix and 1 beaten egg in a bowl and mix well.
- Add 1 cup milk and mix until well blended.
- Stir in 1 tablespoon vegetable oil and mix until well blended.
- Grease a small cast-iron skillet. Heat the skillet until the grease is very hot.
- Pour the corn bread mixture into the skillet.
- Bake at 400 degrees for 20 minutes or until a wooden pick inserted in the center comes out clean.

Powdered buttermilk may be substituted for the milk. Mix according to the package directions to make one cup.

Yield: 8 servings

winter

Pancake mix

1 1/4 cups flour
1/4 cup sugar
1 teaspoon (heaping) baking powder
1 teaspoon baking soda
1/8 teaspoon salt

- Combine the flour, sugar, baking powder, baking soda and salt in a bowl and mix well.
- Store in an airtight container in a cool, dry place.

To prepare Pancakes:
- Combine the mix, 1 beaten egg, 1 1/4 cups buttermilk and 1/4 cup vegetable oil in a large bowl and mix well.
- Spoon about 1/4 cup of the batter onto a hot, lightly greased griddle. Cook until the edges are brown and turn the pancake. Cook until golden brown on both sides.
- Serve with desired toppings.

Yield: 8 to 10 pancakes

Fruit and honey jam

PACKAGE THIS JAM WITH PANCAKE OR BISCUIT MIX AND A COUNTRY HAM FOR A BREAKFAST GIFT. PEACH IS AN ESPECIALLY DELICIOUS FLAVOR TO USE FOR THE JAM.

1 cup honey
¾ cup jam (any flavor)
¼ cup orange juice

- Combine the honey, jam and orange juice in a bowl and mix until well blended.
- Chill, covered, until serving time.
- Serve with biscuits, toast or pancakes.

Yield: 2 cups

winter

Hummingbird cake

THIS CAKE FREEZES WELL. BAKE IN MINIATURE LOAF PANS TO MAKE SEVERAL INDIVIDUAL CAKES FOR GIFT GIVING. STORE IN THE FREEZER FOR AN "ON-HAND" GIFT.

3 cups flour
2 cups sugar
1 teaspoon salt
1 teaspoon baking soda
1 teaspoon cinnamon
3 eggs, beaten
1½ cups vegetable oil

1½ teaspoons vanilla extract
1 (8-ounce) can crushed pineapple, drained
1 cup chopped pecans or walnuts
2 cups chopped bananas, mashed
Cream Cheese Frosting
Chopped pecans (optional)

- Combine the flour, sugar, salt, baking soda and cinnamon in a large bowl and mix well.
- Add the eggs and oil and stir until moistened; do not beat.
- Stir in the vanilla, pineapple, 1 cup pecans and bananas; do not beat.
- Spoon into 3 greased and floured 9-inch cake pans.
- Bake at 350 degrees for 25 to 30 minutes or until the cake tests done.
- Cool in the pans for 10 minutes. Remove to wire racks to cool completely.
- Spread the Cream Cheese Frosting between the layers and over the top and side of the cooled cake.
- Sprinkle with chopped pecans if desired.

Yield: 12 servings

Cream cheese frosting

16 ounces cream cheese, softened
1 cup (2 sticks) margarine, softened

2 (1-pound) packages confectioners' sugar
2 teaspoons vanilla extract

- Beat the cream cheese and margarine in a mixing bowl until well blended.
- Add the confectioners' sugar and beat until light and fluffy.
- Add the vanilla and beat until of spreading consistency.

Chocolate chip cookies

2 cups (4 sticks) butter, softened
2 cups each sugar and packed brown sugar
1 teaspoon salt
2 teaspoons baking soda
1 teaspoon baking powder
4 eggs
2 teaspoons vanilla extract
5 cups rolled oats (finely ground in a blender)
4 cups flour
4 cups (24 ounces) chocolate chips
3 cups chopped nuts

- Beat the butter, sugar and brown sugar in a mixing bowl until light and fluffy.
- Add the salt, baking soda and baking powder and mix well. Beat in the eggs and vanilla.
- Add the oats and flour gradually, mixing well after each addition.
- Stir in the chocolate chips and nuts.
- Drop by large spoonfuls onto cookie sheets.
- Bake at 375 degrees for 6 to 8 minutes.

You may prepare the cookie batter and freeze until needed.

Yield: 10 dozen

Sand art brownies

THIS MAKES A GREAT GIFT FOR THE YOUNG CHEF.

2/3 teaspoon salt
1/2 cup plus 2 tablespoons self-rising flour
2/3 cup packed brown sugar
1/2 cup self-rising flour
1/2 cup baking cocoa
2/3 cup sugar
1/2 cup chocolate chips
1/2 cup white chocolate chips
Pecans or walnuts
3 eggs, beaten
2/3 cup vegetable oil
1 tablespoon vanilla extract

- Layer the salt, 1/2 cup plus 2 tablespoons self-rising flour, brown sugar, 1/2 cup self-rising flour, baking cocoa, sugar, chocolate chips and white chocolate chips in a 1-quart glass jar.
- Fill the jar with pecans.
- Seal with a tight-fitting lid and attach a gift tag with the preparation instructions.

To prepare Sand Art Brownies:
- Pour the mix into a large bowl.
- Add the eggs, oil and vanilla and mix until well blended (about 40 strokes).
- Pour into a greased 9×9-inch baking pan.
- Bake at 350 degrees for 27 to 29 minutes. Do not overbake.

Yield: 1 1/2 dozen

Forever ambers

1 pound orange slice candy
2 (14-ounce) cans sweetened condensed milk
2 (7-ounce) cans flaked coconut
1 teaspoon vanilla extract
1 teaspoon orange extract
1 cup chopped pecans
Confectioners' sugar

- Chop the orange slices into small pieces in a large bowl.
- Combine the sweetened condensed milk, coconut, vanilla and orange extract in a bowl and mix well.
- Stir in the pecans.
- Pour over the orange slice pieces.
- Spread onto a greased baking pan with sides.
- Bake at 275 degrees for 30 to 40 minutes. Let cool slightly.
- Scoop out the candy with a spoon and shape into small balls.
- Roll in confectioners' sugar.
- Store in an airtight container.

To make chopping the orange slice candy easier, try using a sharp knife that has been dipped in warm water. You may also try using kitchen shears. This helps to reduce the stickiness of the candy.

Yield: 7 dozen

Buckeyes

1 cup (2 sticks) margarine, melted
1 cup peanut butter
1 (1-pound) package confectioners' sugar
1 teaspoon vanilla extract
2 cups (12 ounces) chocolate chips
½ (10-ounce) block paraffin

- Combine the melted margarine, peanut butter, confectioners' sugar and vanilla in a large bowl and mix until well blended.
- Shape into balls.
- Melt the chocolate chips and paraffin in a double boiler.
- Dip the balls into the melted chocolate mixture with a wooden pick or skewer.
- Place on a waxed paper-lined baking sheet.
- Chill until firm.
- Store in an airtight container in the refrigerator.

You may also melt the chocolate chips and paraffin in a microwave.

For a variation, you may add raisins with the peanut butter.

Yield: 5 dozen

Cocoa rum balls

1 (12-ounce) package vanilla wafers, crushed
1½ cups chopped nuts
¾ cup confectioners' sugar
¼ cup baking cocoa
½ cup light rum
3 tablespoons light corn syrup
Confectioners' sugar to taste

- Combine the crushed vanilla wafers, chopped nuts, ¾ cup confectioners' sugar and baking cocoa in a large bowl.
- Add the rum and corn syrup and mix well.
- Shape into 1-inch balls.
- Roll in confectioners' sugar to taste to coat.
- Store in an airtight container in the refrigerator for 2 to 3 days.
- Roll again in confectioners' sugar before serving if desired.

Yield: 4 dozen

winter

Microwave peanut brittle

1 cup sugar
1 cup unsalted peanuts
1/8 teaspoon salt
1/2 cup light corn syrup
1 teaspoon margarine
1 teaspoon vanilla extract
1/2 teaspoon baking soda

- Combine the sugar, peanuts, salt and corn syrup in a microwave-safe bowl and mix well.
- Cook on High for 4 minutes, stirring after 2 minutes.
- Stir thoroughly and cook on High for 3 minutes.
- Add the margarine and vanilla and mix well.
- Stir in the baking soda very quickly.
- Pour onto a greased baking sheet.
- Let cool before breaking into bite-size pieces.

Yield: 2 cups

Peanut brittle

THE KEY TO MAKING THIS CANDY IS TO WORK VERY QUICKLY. ASSEMBLE ALL YOUR INGREDIENTS AHEAD OF TIME AND HAVE WITHIN REACH WHILE WORKING.

1/4 cup (1/2 stick) butter
1 cup sugar
1/2 cup light corn syrup
2 cups peanuts
1 teaspoon (heaping) baking soda

- Melt the butter in a cast-iron skillet over high heat.
- Add the sugar and corn syrup and cook until the sugar dissolves, stirring constantly.
- Add the peanuts and mix well.
- Cook until caramel colored.
- Stir in the baking soda very quickly.
- Pour onto a greased baking sheet.
- Let cool before breaking into bite-size pieces.

Yield: 1 1/2 pounds

winter

Peppermint stick sauce

PACKAGE THIS SAUCE IN AN AIRTIGHT CONTAINER WITH CAKE OR HOT CHOCOLATE MIX FOR A FUN WINTERTIME GIFT.

1 cup finely crushed peppermint candies
½ cup heavy cream
½ cup marshmallow creme

- Combine the crushed peppermint candies, cream and marshmallow creme in a medium saucepan.
- Cook over medium-high heat until the candy is melted and the mixture is smooth, stirring occasionally.
- Pour into an airtight container.
- Store in the refrigerator until serving time.
- Serve warm over ice cream or cake.

You may also add 1 to 2 teaspoons of the sauce to hot chocolate or coffee.

Yield: 2 cups

Holiday scent

PACKAGE ALL THE INGREDIENTS, EXCEPT THE WATER, IN A SMALL
SAUCEPAN WITH INSTRUCTIONS AND GIVE AS A HOLIDAY HOSTESS GIFT.

1 quart water
3 cinnamon sticks
3 bay leaves
1/4 cup whole cloves
1/2 to 1 lemon, sliced
1/2 to 1 orange, sliced

- Combine the water, cinnamon sticks, bay leaves,
  cloves, lemon slices and orange slices in a
  saucepan and mix well. Bring to a boil.
- Reduce the heat and simmer for as long as
  desired for the scent to fill the house.
- Check often and add additional water as needed.

*The mixture may be stored in an airtight container
in the refrigerator and re-used, adding additional
water as needed.*

Yield: 4 to 5 cups

Gift ideas

Baskets, Bottles, and Bags

Inexpensive baskets (even peach baskets) can be used for gift giving. To add another dimension of warmth, spray paint the basket to match your recipients' decor. Theme baskets are a great idea. A beverage basket could include mugs, wine glasses, hot chocolate, spiced tea and coffeecino mixes, ingredients for "The Recipe," and cocktail napkins.

Bottles and jars are another way to package goodies. Canning jars, soft drink bottles, and wine bottles are the perfect container. Tie the neck of the jar or bottle with raffia, ribbons, a bandana, or swatch of cloth and the package is wrapped. Personalize these using etching creme to add initials or designs. Fill the jars with a drink mix or Sand Art Brownie mix. The bottles can be filled with multicolored popcorn kernels and topped off with a cork or bottle stopper.

Gift bags can be used in many ways. They come in a variety of sizes and designs for every season or occasion. Any item can be placed within the bag and topped with tissue paper. Add curling ribbon and the gift is ready for giving. As an added bonus, your recipient can reuse the bag. Better yet, make your own designer gift bags. Purchase lunch-size (or any size) plain brown or white bags and punch holes at the top (on each side). String yarn or ribbon through the holes to make handles. Stencil, paint, or draw on the bags to personalize them.

Index

Index

About the illustrator

Beulah Jean Hill Crownover began painting seriously when she was fifty-nine. Although Beulah Jean started painting as a young girl, life got in the way and art took a backseat. For the past ten years, however, painting has come to the forefront in her life. Mrs. Crownover still considers herself an amateur, and the majority of her work is given as gifts. She has also written and illustrated a book with stories from her childhood entitled *Beular Jean*.

Marvelous Morsels

Unique food gifts for year-round giving

Maggie Ruth Smith
1553 Fountain Grove Road
Morrison, Tennessee 37357
931-723-0205
e-mail: mcmkidd@ficom.net

Please send me _____ copies of *Marvelous Morsels* at $14.95 each $ _____

Postage and handling at $3.95 each $ _____

Tennessee residents add 8.25% sales tax $ _____

Total $ _____

Name _____

Street Address _____

City _____ State _____ Zip Code _____

(____) _____ (____) _____
Daytime Telephone Nighttime Telephone

Please make check or money order payable to: Maggie R. Smith

Sorry, credit cards not accepted.